THE LIBERATED GRANDMOTHER

HOW TO BE
A SUCCESSFUL
GRANDMOTHER
WHILE LIVING
YOUR OWN LIFE
AS A FREE AND
HAPPY WOMAN

THE
Liberated
Grandmother

Dorothy C. Finkelhor, Ph.D.

author of *How to Make Your Emotions Work for You*

ORDER BOOKS DIRECTLY FROM AUTHOR
DOROTHY C. FINKELHOR, PH.D.
6590 No. OCEAN BLVD., UNIT 1.,
OCEAN RIDGE, FLORIDA 33435 (TEL: (305) 737-0471)
SEND CHECK OR M.O. $4.95 + $.75 POSTAGE
(IMMEDIATE DELIVERY)

We all love our grandchildren.
This book offers grandmothers
a better chance for a full
life of their own, as well
as being aware of their
grandchildren.

Originally
Published by:
Prince Communications, Inc., New York, N.Y.

Edited by: Harold Prince
Designed by: Paula Wiener

Library of Congress Catalog Card Number 75-8359
International Standard Book Number 0-914302-04-3

Printed and bound in the U.S.A.

The guidelines in this book are based on conclusions drawn from interviews with hundreds of grandmothers throughout the world.

*This book is dedicated to the
memory of my mother, Sarah Wagner
Cimberg, who believed in me and
told me so.*

CONTENTS

Introduction
THE LIBERATED GRANDMOTHER

Even though today's grandmother loves her children and grandchildren, and when occasion demands will do anything in the world for them, she refuses to follow the script for the "typical grandmother" and live at their beck and call.

The liberated grandmother breaks the shackles of typical-grandmother bondage. She sees the typical grandmother role for what it is: a societal pattern of emotional, physical,and financial burdens for her —and she rejects all of it. To her, the pattern of life society forces on grandmothers is a myth: the "grandmother myth."

Why should she be *forced* to assume responsibilities at just that time of her life when nature intended her to be *free?* And she *is* forced when she lives according to the grandmother myth and assumes the typical-grandmother role.

This is the first book ever written on grandmother liberation. It describes for the first time: what the grandmother myth is and how it aborts the natural emotional development of a woman toward freedom and self-realization. And how a woman *can* become a *natural* grandmother by recognizing the grandmother myth for the bad scenario for living it is, and refuse to play the self-nullifying role of the typical grandmother—the *un*natural grandmother.

The natural grandmother is free.

Every normal woman goes through pre-determined stages of development: the child, the teenager, the wife, the mother—all with responsibilities she must assume toward her loved ones. That's the way of nature. But eventually—not suddenly—she reaches a point in life when her children are grown, married, self-sufficient, when there are no longer any responsibilities she *must* assume toward anybody. Nature sets her free to turn dreams into reality and transform herself into the human being—the individual like no other individual—she knows she can be.

But how many grandmothers continue to grow into free, happy, self-realized individuals? Not many in our society. For not long after nature sets them free, a grandchild is born and society clamps them in the emotional shackles of the grandmother myth. Society demands they assume a new responsibility: the grandchild. It's the heaviest responsibility of their lives. It's all-consuming. And it consumes the true self of the woman. She no longer can grow into that special person like no other person in the world. She's cast forever in the stereotype role of the typical grandmother, and basically no typical grandmother differs from another. At the time when a woman can become herself, she becomes like ten million other women.

The liberated grandmother guards her freedom zealously, because she knows it's the most precious gift nature has to offer her. She has the right to her own life. She has the right to make long-deferred dreams come true. She has the right to create a new "me" out of all the potentials locked up in her over her long years of responsibilities. Most of all, she has the right to love—*on her own terms*.

Talk to most grandmothers—and I've interviewed hundreds—and once they get past the point of raving about their grandchildren, they admit that loving on terms that they *think* natural is a bone-wearying job. Almost without exception, they told me, "I'm happy to see them come and I am equally happy to see them go. I haven't the energy for them over a long period of time." One grandmother left for work an hour earlier than usual when the children were visiting. "Otherwise, I'd be too washed out to do my job," she told me.

Love does not mean exhaustion.

But the liberated grandmother *will* love her grandchildren. It's unnatural not to. But she will love them not as a typical grandmother, but as her *own free self*. Love feeds on freedom. She will be a better grandmother because she will be a fulfilled woman. She will reject none of her loved ones. She will only reject the degrading and depersonalizing role of the typical grandmother.

She'll do this without guilt. True love is guilt-free. Typical-grandmother love means unending guilt: How can a grandmother give more than she's capable of? And when she can't she's guilt-ridden.

Free from guilt, free from bondage to the typical grandmother image, the liberated grandmother is free to grow toward self-fulfillment. That growth is not only natural, it's necessary for a happy mind in a healthy body. Growth is the constant development of talents, capacities, creativity, wisdom and character; and when it occurs, particularly in the later years of life, the overall change in a woman is profound. The self-fulfilling woman will see things differently, think differently; emotions and motives will alter; her attitude towards others will shift toward greater respect for them, her attitude to herself toward self-esteem. The self-fulfilling woman will watch with wonder as her potentialities come to complete development, and her inner nature expresses itself freely.

The liberated grandmother, unlike the younger liberated women, can achieve her goals, because she's naturally free to do so. Denied liberation for most of her life, the liberated grandmother can become the *true liberated woman*. The guilt-ridden and basically unhappy existence of a typical grandmother, whose psyche is warped, suppressed and denied, is a sad substitute for this miraculous adventure in living.

The liberated grandmother, revitalized by her inner transformation, will look better, live healthier and longer, glow with serenity.

Liberation, for a grandmother, means *life*.

Part I

RATE YOURSELF AS A GRANDMOTHER

HOW DO YOU RATE AS A GRANDMOTHER?

A one-minute test

	YES	NO
1. Do you consider yourself a *typical* grandmother?	—	—
2. Do you feel it's your duty to pass on all your experiences in child-rearing to your children?	—	—
3. Do you try to impose your ideas on your children because "Grandma knows best"?	—	—
4. When you see your children doing something wrong for your grandchildren, do you step in to set things "right"?	—	—
5. Do you attempt to "bring up your grandchildren" by telling them "to do things that's best for them"?	—	—
6. Is it your job as a grandmother to teach your children "the graces"?	—	—
7. If it's a question of your approval or their parents', should it be *your* approval your grandchildren should look for?	—	—
8. Since you're a good mother, does that mean you're a good grandmother?	—	—

14

9. Do you spend "endless" amounts of time selecting toys, books and phonograph records for your grandchildren? ___ ___

10. Do you feel it's your duty to give money gifts to your grandchildren? ___ ___

11. When your children ask you to do something—anything—for your grandchildren, do you always do it? or feel guilty if you don't? ___ ___

12. Do you feel you should express your love for your grandchildren as intensely as you did for your children? ___ ___

13. Do you believe you must live near your children so you can be helpful? ___ ___

14. Do you regard yourself as the "perfect baby-sitter" —and always available? ___ ___

15. Do you feel obliged to let your grandchildren visit you anytime, and stay as long as their parents let them? ___ ___

16. Do you feel it's your duty to play with your grandchildren? ___ ___

17. When you take care of your grandchildren, do you assume full responsibility for them? ___ ___

18. Do you believe holidays are always happy times—and all the children and grandchildren should always come to grandma's? ___ ___

19. Is it your opinion that once a grandchild is born, it's only natural that your husband should take second place? ___ ___

20. Do you believe that your sex life is over once you become a grandmother? ___ ___

21. Do you enjoy being called "Grandma" by strangers
and relatives other than your grandchildren?   —   —

§   §

Here's How to Rate Yourself:

If you answered *any* of the questions, "YES," your Grandmother
Rating is UNsuccessful. The more YESses you checked off, the more
UNsuccessful you are as a grandmother. In the following pages you'll
find the surprising reasons why . . . and how you can break away from
the grandmother myth and become a *successful liberated grandmother*
—starting today.

Part II

THE "GRANDMOTHER MYTH": IT COULD RUIN THE BEST YEARS OF YOUR LIFE

THE "GRANDMOTHER MYTH": IT COULD RUIN THE BEST YEARS OF YOUR LIFE

In our society, most grandmothers believe all the answers to the questionnaire you've just taken should be "Yes." They are the victims of the "grandmother myth."

They believe they're *unnatural* grandmothers if they don't say "Yes" to those 21 demands on their emotions, time, energy and money, which our society expects from them as proof that they love their grandchildren.

But nothing could be more unnatural than those demands which trap the grandmother into a straitjacket of obligations.

Nature never intended you to show your grandparental love by shouldering a heavy load of burdens and responsibilities.

Nature intends you to be *free* after your children are grown. That means free to give your love on *your* terms, and your terms alone. There are no rules for loving. Love dies in a straitjacket.

Then how do you demonstrate your love for your grandchildren— a love which every grandmother feels instinctively?

By feeling free to follow your natural instincts.

When you do, you'll find your love easy to express.

For example, to teach your grandchildren about life's continuity, and the pleasure and wisdom that comes in growing older, is one of the finest natural expressions of a grandmother's love. What a paltry gift baby-sitting seems by comparison!

Your gifts of love freely expressed will be of inestimable value to your grandchildren. For *those* gifts they'll remember you lovingly forever. Love freely given means happiness for you and your grandchildren.

But you can't give love freely when you're bound by the rules, when you must say "Yes" to the restrictions our society places on you as a grandmother.

To become a successful liberated grandmother, learn to say "No" to those 21 false, unnatural and harmful demands which make up "the grandmother myth." Saying "No" is easy, because it's natural. And in no time at all, you'll be saying "No," without guilt—and enjoying the happy, free life of a *natural* grandmother.

This Part of the book gives you the guidelines.

TO BECOME A *LIBERATED* GRANDMOTHER
YOU MUST LEARN TO SAY: *"NO!"*
TO BECOMING A *TYPICAL* GRANDMOTHER

1

DO YOU CONSIDER YOURSELF A *TYPICAL* GRANDMOTHER?
The Liberated Grandmother Answers:
"NO!"

May I draw you a portrait of what our society sees as a typical grandmother?

A woman who is:

— not only unselfish but selfless;

— whose grandchildrens' welfare is her overriding interest;

— who fills in at all times when she's needed;

— retires when she's in the way;

— who is loving, wise, and relates the past to the grandchildren;

— whose cookies are the best ever baked;

— a kindly, plump, gray-haired lady always on hand to serve and love;

— the dynamic backbone of the family.

Look at yourself in the mirror of your mind. Does the portrait match? I doubt it. None of us can ever hope to live up to that ideal. It's a myth. It's unreal. There's never been such a grandmother.

Try to live up to the ideal, and you're bound to fail. With failure, comes guilt feelings. With guilt feelings—unhappiness, resentment, and smoldering dislikes.

Don't think remaking yourself into the typical grandmother must be your goal.

A grandmother *can* be a svelte, well-coiffed business woman. She *can* be a glamorous, dating divorcee. She *can* be any kind of person she wants to be. Did you know there are typical grandmother dolls for sale, stamped out on an assembly line? Do you want to model yourself after a mass-produced image? Or do you want to *be* yourself?

My grandmother never matched the portrait of a typical grandmother, but she was a great grandmother. We enjoyed weekends at her house, although the food wasn't as good as the food we had at home. Actually, *we* took goodies to *grandmother's* house. There were no cookies, but visiting her was a rich experience. She didn't really do much except talk. But *what* talk! She had a wonderful philosophy of life and did an unforgettable job of passing it on to us. She told us stories that stimulated our imagination.

When there was sickness or trouble, she was the calm center in the storm.

Above all, she was her own person. We remember her not as a stereotyped typical grandmother, but as a remarkable human being.

Everyone agrees that grandmothers are wonderful. When there are no grandparents, parents feel their children are seriously deprived. Margaret Mead's prescription for American children is: more grandmothers. But grandmothers are only wonderful when they don't play the role of the typical grandmother. *You* can be a wonderful grandmother when you play the role of —*yourself*.

2

DO YOU FEEL IT'S YOUR DUTY TO PASS ON ALL YOUR EXPERIENCES IN CHILD-REARING TO YOUR CHILDREN?
The Liberated Grandmother Answers: "NO!"

Every mother wants to help her children to live a good life, especially after the grandchildren are born. How does the woman who plays the typical grandmother role do it?

She looks into her own life, and says, "Had I done such-and-such with my own children, everything would have been better." While her children are growing up, she's collecting this inventory of mistakes; and she's just waiting for grandparent-time when she can pass her warnings on to her sons and daughters.

If she does—and most typical grandmothers feel they *must* or they're unnatural grandmothers—then she's making the biggest of all her mistakes.

She can *not* pass on her experiences to *her* children as guidelines for rearing *their* children. *Her* children are different people than she is; the world in which her grandchildren are being brought up is different than the world in which she brought up her children. Her experiences simply don't relate. To impose them on her children is like asking them to solve one jigsaw puzzle with pieces of another.

24

Let's consider what happens when you try to pass on your child-rearing experiences to your daughter. To begin with, she's a different person than you; what's "right" for your personality isn't always "right" for hers. What's more, she has her own home and her own day-to-day encounters; she knows them, understands them, knows how to cope with them; you don't. Most important: Your daughter isn't the child you remember. Marriage and parenthood have changed her.

In marriage, the husband realizes he isn't the sort of person he thought he was; and the daughter, she isn't the sort of person she thought she was. Together the couple forms an entirely new personality unit. I call what happens "one plus one equals one," which means one male child plus one female child equal one set of parents. The grandmother finds that the mother as a member of the "parent unit" is an utterly new person. Whatever relationship the grandmother had with her daughter before her marriage and parenthood no longer exists. Communication on the old wavelengths—and that's all the typical grandmother is tuned into—is only static. For the grandmother to attempt to "get through" produces only frustration for herself and irritation for her daughter.

The situation is much the same if the child is a son.

The *free* grandmother keeps her mistakes—and her successes—in bringing up children to herself. *That's* the way to really help her children live a good life.

3

DO YOU TRY TO IMPOSE YOUR IDEAS ON YOUR CHILDREN BECAUSE "GRANDMA KNOWS BEST"?
The Liberated Grandmother Answers: "NO!"

You cannot transfer experience from one generation to another. The conditions are different, the children are different, the parents are different. Then what makes you think that becoming a grandparent gives you the right to impose your ideas on your children?

You think so because it's part of our modern "grandmother myth." You've been brainwashed by our society into believing that if your children would only listen to you, your children's children would be reared better and your children would have a better life. If you swallow this myth, your life could be a kind of "hell on earth" every time you see your children handling your grandchildren differently than you would have done had they been your children. It seems to you that your children are on the way to re-living your mistakes, and you must step in to set them straight—even if it means one emotional scene after another.

The truth is, you can not set your children straight based on your own experience of child-rearing. And what other practical knowledge on the subject have you? Face it, you have no background that qualifies you to take over the total rearing of your grandchildren. Get used to that idea and your days of "hell on earth" will be over.

The liberated grandmother understands that her children must have the freedom she commands for herself. The daughter, who has the responsibility for rearing the children, must be left free to establish her own identity. She must be free, in the light of that identity, to think—while changing diapers and preparing food—of the big question, "What is the best way to rear my child to become a mature person?" She must be free, in unison with her husband, to meet and solve the problems of child-rearing against a background of today's living world, not the dead world of the grandmother's youth.

Let your children learn the job of child-rearing their own way—and you'll find yourself free of a false and harmful obligation. And they'll find themselves free to do the job nature intended for them: to bring up their children to an adulthood of mature happiness. Do that and you'll be a grandma who *really* knows best. Don't do it, and your life could be a kind of "hell on earth" every time you see your children handling your grandchildren differently than you would.

4

WHEN YOU SEE YOUR CHILDREN DOING SOMETHING WRONG FOR YOUR GRANDCHILDREN DO YOU STEP IN TO SET THINGS "RIGHT"?
The Liberated Grandmother Answers: "NO!"

The grandmother myth makes it *your* responsibility to step in and correct the mother when you think she's doing something wrong in the rearing of your grandchild. But when you take over the authority to decide right from wrong, you're giving the mother a "cop-out." That's the purpose of this aspect of the grandmother myth: to give the parents freedom from responsibility—and hang that responsibility on *your* shoulders.

But, as pointed out in the last section, you really don't know if *anything* about modern child-rearing is right or wrong. You're *not* neglecting your duty by keeping quiet. You're really carrying out your true duty as a grandmother by letting the parents bring up the children. When you assume *their* burdens, you're crippling them emotionally as parents and as human beings.

Let the parents decide what's right or wrong for your grandchildren.

When your opinion is asked, give it freely. But *never* try to coerce or persuade your children to accept your decision. As the years go by, you'll be surprised to find how many of your decisions would have turned out wrong anyway.

And, remember, the less you interfere, the more mental freedom *you'll* have to pursue your own interests and create your own identity. *That's* the right way of seeing that things go right—for *you*. When you don't step in to right a "wrong," you're taking the right step to achieve good relationships with your children and enduring happiness for yourself.

5

DO YOU ATTEMPT TO "BRING UP YOUR GRANDCHILDREN" BY TELLING THEM "TO DO THINGS THAT ARE BEST FOR THEM"?
The Liberated Grandmother Answers: "NO!"

Certainly, the grandmother has an educational role to fill for her grandchildren. But she doesn't fill that role successfully when she tells her grandchildren, "Do *this* or do *that* because it's the thing that's best for you." How does a grandmother, who was a child decades ago, know what's best for today's child?

Nothing is more destructive than trying to make a grandchild over in the grandmother's image of herself as a child—an image that faded away two generations ago.

Do you understand now why the myth which assigns you the duty of telling your grandchildren what's best for them to do is false and harmful?

The liberated grandmother lets her grandchild decide what he or she wants to do in the grandchild's own good time. The grandmother's patience will be rewarded by watching her grandchildren grow freely into mature individuals. I know of few joys of grandmotherhood that are greater.

6

IS IT YOUR JOB AS A GRANDMOTHER TO TEACH YOUR GRANDCHILDREN "THE GRACES"?
The Liberated Grandmother Answers: "NO!"

It is part of the grandmother myth that typical grandmothers are ideally prepared to teach children "the graces"—the good manners and behavior of civilized living. But today's typical grandmother learned her graces two generations back when we lived in a different world. The patterns of living have changed radically. What were the standards of good behavior in the grandmother's youth—etiquette, it was called— might be looked upon as an unrealistic "put on" by today's youth.

The typical grandmother is ill-equipped to take on this specialized teaching chore. The mother's ideas and the grandmother's ideas— separated by the generation gap—are bound to clash. Imagine, for example, trying to teach old-fashioned good manners to a child whose mother insists that "good manners are inhibiting."

The liberated grandmother, on the other hand, knows that each generation creates its own standards of behavior—some generations, as those of the 50s and 60s, more dramatically than others. Those are not her values, and she knows she's unable to teach them. But she just doesn't throw her hands up. She knows she can teach good manners best by not teaching at all in the usual sense, but by leading her life with consideration and thoughtfulness to others, which is the essence of good manners in any generation. Her example will certainly leave its mark on her grandchildren.

If you desire your grandchildren to learn the ways to behave toward other people—ways which you clearly believe are necessary to their future well-being—don't teach, demonstrate. When your behavior is a living display of better living, imitation is sure to follow.

§   §

Grandchildrens' bad manners distress a grandmother, but if she were to correct them overtly she would be hurting her daughter or daughter-in-law, and creating a new family tension. When a grandmother criticizes the manners of her grandchildren, she is really criticizing the mother. It's the mother who is responsible, in the main, for her children's behavior. The liberated grandmother eliminates clashes between members of the family by refusing to usurp the responsibility of the mother.

7

IF IT'S A QUESTION OF YOUR APPROVAL OR THEIR PARENTS', SHOULD IT BE *YOUR* APPROVAL YOUR GRANDCHILDREN LOOK FOR?
The Liberated Grandmother Answers: "NO!"

The grandmother who "takes over" is usually a destructive grandmother.

She's in command of *another* family, or *two* other families, or *three* other families, or *more*.

That may give her a heady feeling of power. But does it work? Does it build happy fulfilled lives for her grandchildren and their parents? Seldom, if ever.

Read the book *Franklin and Eleanor* by Joseph Lash, in which he details how difficult the grandmother—FDR's mother—made life, not only for Eleanor, but for her children. When Eleanor told her children not to do something, they would just go ahead and do it, yelling, "Grandmother approved." FDR's mother actually told her grandchildren, "Your mother is a bore. But never mind, you're *my* children."

The grandmother is not equipped by experience to bring up her grandchildren; her experience is composed of obsolete shadows out of the past. Nature never intended the grandmother to do the work of the mother.

What's more, the grandmother who is forced by the social pressures of the grandmother myth to "take over" probably bears resentments, angers and guilts because of a responsibility she never wanted. Such a person must have a bad influence on her family.

You don't want to be that kind of grandmother. It's easy not to be. Just remember, you're *free* of the responsibility of heading up any more families. Make it clear to the grandchildren from the start that it's *their mother* who makes the decisions, not you. And—*really* approve the mother's decisions.

You'll find that mother and children will approve of *you* more, when they know that you don't expect to be asked for your approval.

8

SINCE YOU'RE A GOOD MOTHER, DOES THAT MEAN YOU'RE A GOOD GRANDMOTHER?
The Liberated Grandmother Answers: "NO!"

The grandmother myth would have you believe that becoming a grandmother is simply an extension of becoming a mother. Believe that, and you take over the mother's duties and responsibilities for your grandchild. I've already pointed out that, while this may be often a "blessing" for the grandchild's mother (she has somebody doing *her* work), it's *un*natural. It's harmful to the mother, the child, and the grandmother.

The mother has her natural role to play. The grandmother has hers.

The grandmother's role is different than that of the mother's.

Just what *is* that role?

Up to now, the grandmother's role has been defined by the "grandmother myth." This book exposes that myth for what it is—a false set of demands that reduces the grandmother to the status of a servant, who not only receives no pay but works beyond her capacities.

The *true* grandmother's role in our society is spelled out in the pages you've already read and the pages ahead of you. To prepare for that role—and for the happiness and freedom that go with it—you must first learn to say *"NO!"* to all the false requirements society demands of the "typical grandmother" (Part II)—and then learn to say *"YES!"* to the brand-new *Grandmother's Bill of Rights* (Part V).

If you're already a grandmother, start shedding your "typical grandmother" role *now*. There's no time to lose. If you're not yet a grandmother, it's never too early to start preparing. Learn how to be a liberated grandmother *now*—and avoid headaches, heartaches and muscle aches later on, while enjoying the earned love of your children and grandchildren—and the happiness of establishing your own identity as a person.

9

DO YOU SPEND "ENDLESS" AMOUNTS OF TIME SELECTING TOYS, BOOKS AND PHONOGRAPH RECORDS FOR YOUR GRANDCHILDREN?
The Liberated Grandmother Answers: "NO!"

The typical grandmother is a 365-day-a-year Santa Claus. But unlike Santa Claus she doesn't ask what the children want. *She* decides, without even consulting the parents. That means she has to spend hours, days sometimes, shopping for toys, books, records. It's exhausting, but the sacrifice is good for the children—and that's what being a grandmother is all about, isn't it?

Is it?

What does a grandmother really know about what a child wants? I like to tell the story of a five-year-old whose grandmother took him to visit an uncle who owned a toy store. The grandmother wasn't well off financially, and she had been feeling guilty because her presents to her grandson had been inexpensive. But today she'd make amends —in a big way. The uncle was a generous and understanding man, and he'd arranged with the grandmother to let the little boy have anything he wanted in the store, "as a gift from your grandma, youngster." The store was brimming with toys of all kinds, including extravagantly expensive imports. The costliest item in the shop was a sports car, scaled down to seat a five-year-old.

"I want *that,*" said the youngster.

"The sports car?" beamed his grandmother.

"No, *that,*" said the youngster pointing to an item in a glass case near the sports car.

"*That!*" cried the grandmother in shocked disbelief.

The uncle reached into the case and gave the little boy the present he desired most. It was a twenty-five-cent rubber ball.

Want more proof that wearing yourself out deciding on gifts for your grandchildren is all wrong? Look at your gift-giving from the mother's viewpoint:

Toys, books and records are learning devices. The mother, who has fairly definite ideas on the learning process, should be consulted before you make a selection. Bringing the wrong kind of gift, from the mother's viewpoint, could be a disruptive influence in the household.

The liberated grandmother feels free to give a gift or not give a gift to her grandchildren. When she does give a gift, she attempts to make certain that it's something the child really wants and the mother approves of. A little more understanding of your grandchildren and a little more talk with their mother can free you of the burdens and guilts of continual gift-giving and gift-giving decisions. That's a load off your mind, off your feet, and off your pocketbook.

10

DO YOU FEEL IT'S YOUR DUTY TO GIVE MONEY GIFTS TO YOUR GRANDCHILDREN?
The Liberated Grandmother Answers: "NO!"

Regular money-giving is a characteristic of the "typical grand-mother." The grandmother myth makes it the duty of every grand-mother to shower cash on her grandchildren—often, whether she can afford to or not.

As for all other aspects of the grandmother myth, there's a very hard-headed (I almost wrote "hard-hearted") reason behind this one: The grandmother is "easy-pickings." The brainwashed grandmother is expected to give and give—after all, isn't she supposed to give her *all* for her grandchildren? Five-dollar bills, ten-dollar bills, and frequently *large* sums slip away from her savings. Even if she's well off, her bank balance may begin to dip at a time of her life when *her* family's earnings are dipping, too. Is *that* fair?

Pity the poor grandmother who gives and gives and really can't afford to, just to keep her status as a "typical grandmother." Is *that* fair?

Pity the even poorer grandmother who is unable to give any cash and who is ridden by guilt and inferiority because of her poverty. As a grandmother, she drearily considers herself a failure. Is *that* fair?

And even if her family's earnings are going up, it still isn't fair to ask her to become a one-woman welfare state. No matter how much money a grandmother has, she has the right to use that money as she pleases.

When you get into the habit of giving cash regularly to your grandchildren *as a duty,* you're being unfair to yourself, and you're doing yourself harm.

You're also harming your children and your grandchildren.

Money gifts can become a form of bribery. No good relationship was ever established on the basis of bribery. As long as they think, even in the back of their heads, that you're trying to buy their love, you won't get it.

What's more, after a while, your children will regard your "bribes" as a form of social security—to be expected on a steady basis. If for any reason at all, you can't keep up your payments, you'll be faced with a sudden and frigid withdrawal of love. The reaction will be virtually automatic, and the children will be as shocked by their actions as you are—leaving permanent wounds on all.

Once your grandchildren are old enough to appreciate the value of money, they'll regard your "duty" payments as their due. When money is force-fed on a steady basis without it being earned in any way, the grandchild could grow up thinking there's always some "fairy grandmother" around, ready to shower him or her with greenbacks. That's only one step toward the attitude of "the world owes me a living." And since the world *doesn't,* your grandchild might very well grow up unable to cope with the basic problem of earning one's keep. Whose fault? *Yours*—if you're a "typical grandmother."

§   §

Money gifts to your grandchildren should be given freely—when you want to, when you feel they're needed—and only when you're able to. If it's in your power to give your grandchildren a large check for something *you* know they couldn't get any other way—private school tuition, music or dance classes, a summer camp, a trip abroad

—and you can do it without hurting *your* pocketbook, do it. It's a valid expression of love. Your children and grandchildren will love you for it.

But don't over-give. Don't give more to your grandchildren than your children approve of. That erodes the grandchildren's respect for their parents (this *is* a money-oriented society). If you want to make a magnificent financial gesture, do it in such a way that the parents are not hurt.

11

WHEN YOUR CHILDREN ASK YOU TO DO SOMETHING—ANYTHING— FOR YOUR GRANDCHILDREN, DO YOU ALWAYS DO IT OR FEEL GUILTY IF YOU DON'T?
The Liberated Grandmother Answers: "NO!"

A grandmother I interviewed told me her daughter had asked her to take care of her infant baby. "I simply did not feel capable," the grandmother complained. "I didn't feel I could assume the responsibility of taking care of an infant."

She said she was afraid something might happen to the child. "I have the feeling that if you take care of your grandchild and something happens, it's worse than if something happens to your own child. At least your own child is yours to do with, but this child isn't yours.

"I would do anything for my children—and for my grandchildren— but I had to turn my daughter down, and I feel so guilty."

One of the purposes of this book is to remove the guilt from being a grandmother. You only feel guilt when you try to live up to the role our society expects of a typical grandmother. But that role is a false one. It requires you to give your all for your grandchildren—all the time. But there's no *natural reason* in the world why you *should* be required to do so.

You're *not* the grandchild's mother. The love of a mother for a child is so great, that if the child asks the mother for something—anything—the mother will say "Yes," if a "Yes" is at all possible. When the mother asks you to do something for her grandchild with no answer expected except "Yes," she's passing her role as a mother on to you. It's not fair. It's not natural.

What nature intended for your golden years is for you to use your own time as you see fit. Before your children were grown, you probably didn't have the leisure and the money (children *are* expensive) to do the things you wanted to do to develop *yourself* as a human being. Now's your chance. But *not* if you let yourself become a mother again.

The true grandmother gives of herself and her time when she feels she's making a contribution to her grandchild's or her children's welfare that no one else can make. She's always at stand-by, for example, to meet emergencies. Grandmothers are willing to step in and do all that they can in critical situations. That's the kind of natural dependence on each other that keeps a family together. But emergencies are rare events.

Your job is to free yourself of all the unnatural restrictions placed on you the day you became a grandmother. Only when you're free can you become a true individual. And only a true individual can be a successful grandmother. For only then will she be able to bring the best of *herself* to her grandchildren—which is one of the finest ways of expressing love I know.

"I love my grandchildren, but I'm *not* willing to do *anything* in the world for them" is the motto of the grandmother who truly loves. (What is *necessary* to do, a liberated grandmother always does naturally.)

12

DO YOU FEEL YOU MUST EXPRESS YOUR LOVE FOR YOUR GRANDCHILDREN AS INTENSELY AS YOU DID FOR YOUR CHILDREN?
The Liberated Grandmother Answers: "NO!"

There isn't a normal parent who wouldn't "give up everything" or "do anything" or "give their all" for their children. That's natural. The child's life is an extension of the parents'; and how, then, can a parent fail to do less than his or her utmost for the child? It's in the act of giving one's all, of sacrificing to the limit, that the mother expresses her love for her child.

Can there be the same expression of love between a grandmother and her grandchild?

At first glance, it would appear that the answer is "Yes." Mothers of married children can hardly wait to become grandmothers. It's one of the cornerstone events of their mature years. When the child is born, they are eager to give of themselves. And they *do*. They *over*-do. When a parent objects, "Oh, mother, you're doing too much!" the grandmother's answer is, "It's all right, I love doing it."

Then nature steps in and says to the grandmother, "You're not as young as you once were." No matter how alive a grandmother seems, and how full of zip and energy, age takes its toll. The grandmother just isn't capable of doing all the things she wants to do, let alone *over-do*, without fatigue setting in fast and hard. At this point, the grandmother should begin to ease off. But she can't. She's been caught in a trap. Here's what's happened:

The child's mother has become dependent upon the grandmother. To meet the mother's demands, the grandmother pushes herself harder and harder. But the harder she pushes, the greater the fatigue. As the grandmother's energy-level sinks, the energy-level of the growing youngster she's taking care of zooms. The grandmother finds herself more and more unable to cope. Besides, virtually all of her time is now devoted to the grandchild. Where's the time to do all the things she wants to do for *herself*? Where's the time to develop *herself* as a human being? It's all gone—her time, her energy, her freedom. The grandmother has *truly* given her all.

Now the grandmother feels resentment; she doesn't like to be taken for granted. And she feels frustrated because she's not able to fight off her natural fatigue—and really isn't "up" to doing all the things required of her. Grandmothers say, "I love my grandchildren and I'd give them my all"—but deep in their hearts, they realize they *can't* give their all. And that means guilt.

What a burden to bear for falling into the trap of believing a grandmother has to express her love for her grandchildren as intensively as she did for her own children. That belief is a myth that could destroy the grandmother, and hurt the parents and the grandchild.

A grandmother can not—by the very nature of things—take the place of a mother. A grandmother's love is different than a mother's love. A grandmother, unlike a mother, isn't called upon by nature to give her "all" to express her love for her grandchildren.

A grandmother's love is expressed quite differently. It begins with learning to love yourself by becoming a free individual. Then your love for your grandchildren will be expressed freely—in hundreds of charming ways that will surprise even you. The expression of your love will flow *naturally* when you have the time, the energy, and the freedom from duress to be the kind of person you're proud of being. You can only be *that* person when you admit you can *not* love your grandchildren as intensely as you did your children.

13

DO YOU BELIEVE YOU MUST LIVE NEAR YOUR CHILDREN SO YOU CAN BE HELPFUL?
The Liberated Grandmother Answers: "NO!"

One of the grandmothers I interviewed referred to herself as an "unnatural grandmother" because she was moving to Spain. She said, "A good grandmother would not do that. She would stay home and help her child rear the grandchildren."

I know that's the way most grandmothers feel who have been hypnotized by the "grandmother myth." This woman *wanted* to go to Spain, felt she would be happy in Spain, and yet she was consumed by guilt. If she had only realized she was *free to go or stay,* she could have made her decision without her terrible mental anguish.

If you decide *to stay* near (or with) your grandchildren, get accustomed to the idea that it's not going to be all love and cookies. Aside from the physical strain—a three-year-old can wear out an athlete—you're going to watch your daughter (more than your son, because she's the homemaker) face the daily struggles of life. Living close by —or worse, in the same home—you see your children struggling through life's day-by-day problems, and the extremely special problems of bringing up children in a world in which moral values are crumbling.

You can't help very much. Your children are fighting their problems on a different battlefield against new enemies and weapons. Your vast experience of victories and defeats in past battles for happiness is of little use in the world your children struggle in.

Live close by, if you like. But make that decision with your eyes open. Realize that your child isn't different from everybody else: she cannot escape the vexing day-by-day problems that beset all of today's parents. And living close by, you cannot escape the day-by-day agony of watching your child suffer through her life with her children.

There's nothing much you can do. Your daughter doesn't really want you as a partner in the rearing of her children. You're not a way out for her problems; you're just in the way.

The liberated grandmother knows that her children must face up to difficult child-rearing situations, and she accepts it as a fact of life. The liberated grandmother, with confidence in her children, knows that they will win more often then they lose—when there's no grandmaternal interference. She knows enough to keep out of the way. That means more joy than sorrow—all the way round.

If keeping out of the way is one key to a better life for your children and your grandchildren, why feel guilty when you feel like migrating? The many thousands of grandparents who have created new lives for themselves among their peers in warmer climates and elsewhere around the world are evidence that a trend exists among grandparents to take care of their own needs as opposed to making themselves available at all times to their children.

Some of the highest praise of grandmothers I've ever heard comes from sons and daughters who live thousands of miles away.

One liberated grandmother who lived more than a continent-width away told us how wonderful it was when her grandchildren came to visit her. "It was marvelous to see them come. And," she added, "it was just as marvelous to see them go." She gives this advice: "Don't live too close to your own children."

That's *her* solution. You can choose to live close by. If you do, be prepared to take the consequences. *You* make the decision.

But sometimes the decision isn't yours to make. In today's mobile economy, children frequently move to a distant part of the country, leaving grandparents behind. This move could break the heart of a typical grandmother. The liberated grandmother is prepared to make the most of the opportunity.

14

DO YOU REGARD YOURSELF AS "THE PERFECT BABY-SITTER"— AND ALWAYS AVAILABLE?
The Liberated Grandmother Answers: "NO!"

What happens when you're asked to baby-sit, and you have something else to do, or you just plain don't feel like it? Chances are, you'll answer "Yes," because if you answer "No," you'll be consumed with guilt. Isn't a grandmother assumed to be the perfect baby-sitter? And isn't a grandmother supposed to be always on call to baby-sit whenever the children telephone?

Nothing could be further from the truth.

In the first place, you're *not* the perfect baby-sitter. Your ideas of bringing up a child will *not* match those of your children; there's a generation gap that's unbridgable. If the parents are "permissive" and you're a disciplinarian, for example—or vice-versa—your baby-sitting could wreak havoc. A professional baby-sitter just *sits*.

In the second place, why do you think you should *always* be available? Don't you understand that when you think this way you've been entrapped by the "grandmother myth"?

And do you know one of the most important reasons why the grandmother myth has existed for years?

To turn you into a super-servant.

There's no facet of the myth that underscores this ugly truth more strongly than "baby sitting." You're supposed to be ready on a minute's notice to baby-sit—no matter whether there's a storm or a blizzard, or if you have other engagements, or if you're indisposed, or if you'd just rather sit home snuggled up to the TV. And you're supposed to perform this incredible service—*free of charge*!

A young mother said to me the other day, "I believe in women getting their freedom," and she's women's lib, "but it's so expensive to get baby-sitters, I'd like to maintain the status of the grandmother as it is."

You know what one of the grandmothers answered that woman? "If you can afford to go to the theater, you can afford a baby-sitter." Good for her!

§   §

Baby-sit only when *you* want to. Your children won't take you for granted—and that means more prestige and self-esteem for you. And, once you've begun to say "No"—realizing that it's best for the grandchildren, the children, and you *to* say "No" more often than "Yes"—your guilt will fall off you like a rain-soaked overcoat. What a grand and glorious feeling of lightheartedness and freedom!

§   §

There's another side to that coin—a bright side. As a liberated grandmother, you'll find yourself saying, "Let's *take* the children,"— and meaning it. You'll do it because you want to, have the energy to, and because you've planned the time you'll spend with them. You won't be doing it because you're driven by guilt.

15

DO YOU FEEL OBLIGATED TO LET YOUR GRANDCHILDREN VISIT YOU ANYTIME, AND STAY AS LONG AS THEIR PARENTS LET THEM?
The Liberated Grandmother Answers: "NO!"

Should a grandmother run a hotel for her grandchildren—open 24 hours a day, 365 days a year—no reservations required?

Absolutely! asserts the grandmother myth.

Nonsense! answers mother nature.

As a grandmother, you have the right to your own feelings. You must understand them well enough to know what you can cope with emotionally, and what you can't. If you just can't put up with a surprise visit from your grandchildren, put your foot down. Say to the parents. "I love the children, but give me a chance to say 'No.'" You'll find the parents will respect you for it, because deep in their hearts they'll agree with you.

Even with the best will in the world, grandparents find extended visits from their grandchildren a mind-and-body-draining experience.

"Growing up" is a long, tedious process for adults to share. Nature meant the sharing to be a job for parents; but even for them it's tiresome on a daily round-the-clock basis. Nature never intended it to be a job for grandmothers, to whom it can be utterly exhausting even when the "growing-up-sharing" comes in small visits.

The liberated grandmother wants to see her grandchildren when *she* wants to see them. She'll enjoy having them when she feels up to it—when she's mentally ready and she's physically fit. And when she's had enough, she'll speak up and say so without a trace of guilt.

That means you've given your "best time" to your little *guests* (*that's* how you should consider them) which makes *them* happy. That means your heart has been lifted by their company without fatigue or strain, which makes *you* happy. And, after they've gone, just consider all the time you have to develop the *true* you quietly, without fearing the shrieks of *un*invited little guests streaking across the threshold of your serenity.

§   §

Remember, though, that visits from your grandchildren can be a joyful occasion that nothing else can really match. Listen to a grandmother whom I interviewed:

"I enjoy being a grandmother even though I'm a long-distance grandmother. Going to a Walt Disney show and lunching and shopping with them, picnicking with them on Grandma's terrific home-made sandwiches, cookies and candy which took hours to prepare, is a special treat for me. Playing their games with them is fun. I love being a grandmother, and I certainly would *not* want to be forgotten. Even though I'm tired and the grandchildren tease me into doing something or going somewhere I don't want to, I go along with their ideas and I find that it's fun to do things for the young, to be with them. I become revitalized. The tiredness is gone. I feel good.

"Another thing. Do you realize how our children's energies are sapped from daily responsibilities, financial problems? They don't have the time or energy to give the kind of relaxed attention that grandmothers can give to their grandchildren. What a grandmother gives her grandchildren is privileged, special attention that makes them tender, loving human beings. Most parents can't give what a grandmother gives. I know that I'm a very special being to my grandchildren.''

But this woman *is* a long-distance grandmother. Her grandchildren visit her once a year. Do I make my point clear?

16

DO YOU FEEL IT'S YOUR *DUTY* TO PLAY WITH YOUR GRANDCHILDREN?
The Liberated Grandmother Answers: "NO!"

The grandmother myth has another role for the grandmother: entertainer. Every mother knows the "horrors" of having a bored child on her hands. What's the easiest way to escape the responsibility of making life interesting for the child? Pass the responsibility on to grandma.

But do you have the energy to keep up with, say, a three-year-old? Few grandmothers do. If you try to play for more than a short time (and I call 30 minutes a *long* time), you'll be mentally and physically exhausted. Sure, that didn't happen with your own children. But that was years and years and years ago, wasn't it? Your children have the stamina *now* that you had *then*. Let *your* children play with *their* children. You—sit by and watch.

Above all, don't feel frustrated or angry with yourself, or consider yourself a bad grandmother, if you find it an effort to play with your grandchildren. Nature never intended you to—except for reasonable periods.

Make your golden years *your* playtime. *Not* your grandchildren's.

§   §

Many grandmothers have delightful skills they'd like to pass on, such as cooking, gardening, sewing, painting, and singing. They do these things well, and would enjoy teaching them to their grandchildren.

17

WHEN YOU TAKE CARE OF YOUR GRANDCHILDREN, DO YOU ASSUME FULL RESPONSIBILITY FOR THEM?
The Liberated Grandmother Answers: "NO!"

"A grandchild was staying with me. Suddenly, I heard her voice upstairs. I dashed up and there she was standing at an open window. Very quietly I picked her up and sat down with her.

"You know what I thought at that moment? I'm ashamed to say it, but I wasn't thinking only of the child's narrow escape. I was also thinking that if anything had happened to her, I would have to go away. Truly, I thought that I would either run away, or I would have to die.

"Because, if something had happened to that child when she was in my care, that would be the worst thing I could do to my daughter."

Another grandparent told me, "One day I lost my grandchild. That is, I went to pick her up at school and we missed one another. I was absolutely frantic. As I was running and looking for her, I thought, it isn't only the child I've hurt, look what I've done to my daughter. I've taken her child from her."

When a grandmother takes care of a child she assumes a gigantic emotional burden. The stress, in many cases, can become unbearable. Is this intensive sense of responsibility justified?

The grandmother myth asserts it is. That's to be expected. The grandmother myth has arisen to shift the burden of some of the more unpleasant parts of child rearing from the parents to the grandparents. But the myth masks this fundamental truth.

It's the parents, and the parents alone, who by nature have the responsibility for the safety of their offspring. The parents are *still* responsible when they place the child in *any*body's hands—and that includes the grandmother's hands.

When a grandmother takes care of a grandchild, she does not assume the parents' responsibility. And, certainly, she doesn't assume the super-responsibility thrust upon her by the grandmother myth. The only responsibility she assumes is to take prudent care of the grandchild—and this is important—*within the limits of her physical and emotional capabilities*. She's never *fully* responsible for the child, in the sense that the parents are.

There are certainly times when you will, quite freely, *want to* take care of your grandchildren. Do so with a free mind. If anything should go wrong, it's not you who bears the full responsibility. Let that simple truth become part of your mental-emotional makeup, and you'll discover a new kind of joy when your grandchildren are in your care.

18

DO YOU BELIEVE HOLIDAYS ARE ALWAYS HAPPY TIMES—AND ALL THE CHILDREN AND GRANDCHILDREN SHOULD ALWAYS COME TO GRANDMA'S?
The Liberated Grandmother Answers: "NO!"

Many psychologists now hold that loneliness is incurable. A holiday is not a happy time for lonely people, even if they have families. If they feel alone *within themselves,* it doesn't make any difference how many people there are around them. People who are basically lonely would rather sleep away the holidays than be confronted by them. Holidays are *not* always happy times.

"I think I know the reason behind the myth that holidays are happy times," one women's lib advocate said to me. "It's up to the *grandmother* to *make* them happy. Cooking. Fussing. Calling up the family. Getting them together. Giving presents. Letting some of the family stay over. Keeping a watch on the grandchildren. You know something," she added, "on holidays the grandmother becomes a cook, good-will ambassador, maitre d', hotel manager. Where does she get the energy? And, besides, she *bankrolls* the whole thing!"

And with all that effort, more often than not, the family holiday party turns out to be less than a happy event.

Disaster No. 1. Let's say everybody who's invited comes. There aren't very many families in which there isn't somebody who doesn't get along with somebody else. Before the party is over, somebody's at loggerheads with somebody; somebody's feelings are hurt. Who's the peacemaker? The grandmother. If she can make peace, she's worn out emotionally. If she can't make peace, she feels it's all her fault, and carries the guilt around with her for weeks.

Disaster No. 2. There's almost always somebody who says, "Sorry, Grandma, we can't come." Since the grandmother myth has elevated attendance at family holiday parties to a sign of homage to the grandmother, failure to attend is, in the words of one typical grandmother, "a slap in the face." Another typical grandmother told me that when her son turned down her Thanksgiving party invitation, she "was never so hurt in her life."

Does any of these hurts, frustrations, guilts, over-exertions, and over-spending make any real sense? They might if it all added up to happiness. But it doesn't.

Make up your mind that holidays are not automatically happy times. (As if happiness could be turned on and off like a faucet.) And keep one thing clear: You're *not* required to have "everybody over to Grandma's for the holidays."

The free grandmother *makes her own holidays* by inviting her family when she wants them, when she's up to fussing over them, and when she's sure the family members she selects will be happier together than apart.

There's an added advantage for the grandmother who puts her foot down to giving holiday parties. She's likely to be invited *out* instead.

§   §

If you take holidays in your stride and don't burden yourself with unnecessary responsibilities, you *could* give a memorable party now and then. Why not? But, remember, it's strictly *your* affair.

19

IS IT YOUR OPINION THAT ONCE A GRANDCHILD IS BORN, IT'S ONLY NATURAL THAT YOUR HUSBAND SHOULD TAKE SECOND PLACE?
The Liberated Grandmother Answers: "NO!"

This is a typical incident:

The grandparents go to the son's house for dinner. After dinner, the grandfather returns to his own home. The grandmother stays, spends the night baby-sitting, and sleeps over.

Fine!—if the grandfather was consulted by his wife and agreed. But he was *not* consulted, and he did *not* agree. It never occurred to the grandmother to ask her husband how he felt. She just assumed her first responsibility was to the grandchild, and "granddad" just had to play second fiddle.

Few grandfathers in a situation like that would have the gumption to say, "I like to sleep in my own home, and I am going to do just that, and I don't appreciate your sleeping elsewhere." But one grandfather I know did, and that set his wife thinking, "*Is* it right to consider my grandchild ahead of my husband?"

I can give her the answer, short and sweet: "It's *not*."

Once your own children are grown, you're *free*. And one aspect of that freedom is to develop your relationship with your husband. In your golden years, there's nothing to stand in the way of spending both your lives by getting to know each other better. When you place your grandchildren ahead of your husband, you're in reality taking them along on your second honeymoon.

That part of the grandmother myth which insists that the grandchildren come first, husband second, really means: you're a servant first, a wife second. No woman wants that. When you realize that it's only a "myth" that's trapping you into neglecting your husband, you're on the road to a bright "new" marriage. It's always better the second time around—whether it's with the same man or a new one.

20

DO YOU BELIEVE THAT YOUR SEX LIFE IS OVER ONCE YOU BECOME A GRANDMOTHER?
The Liberated Grandmother Answers: "NO!"

The "grandmother myth" can be very cruel. In order to tie you down to your grandchild, it tries to divorce you from your husband. "I'm a grandmother now, sex is not important," is what the grandmother myth makes you believe. But look behind the myth, and you'll see that what you're saying to yourself really is: "All my thoughts should be on my grandchild; all my time should be devoted to him or her; my husband just has to fade into the background because he gets in the way of my being a typical grandmother."

But remember, being a typical grandmother by living up to the standards of the grandmother myth, means you're *un*naturally shouldering the responsibilities of your children, becoming a taken-for-granted servant without pay and, often, without thanks.

Don't give up your husband for your grandchildren; when you do, you're playing right into the hands of the "grandmother myth" and giving up one of the best things in your life to enter a life of servitude, anxieties, responsibilities and guilts. You *do* give up your husband when sex takes second place. You also give up some of the happiest moments of your golden years.

Sex lasts for almost the entire lifetime of a woman. Yes, that *is* an established scientific fact. I love to watch elderly couples walking hand-in-hand with the love-light gleaming in their eyes. To them, sex is a beautiful necessity. It should be to every liberated grandmother.

So, when the children call up and say, "Grandma, will you sleep over tonight with the youngsters?" remember, that's not *your* job; it's your children's. Your job—your *joy*—is sleeping with your husband. Say *"No!"* to the kids and *"Yes!"* to him. You'll be saying "Yes" to a fully realized life.

§   §

And while we're on the subject of your sex life as a grandmother, don't ever stop trying to make yourself look attractive and glamorous. You have every right to be as alluring as a teenager has. Remember, *today* is your future. Enjoy every minute of it—as a *fulfilled woman.*

21

DO YOU ENJOY BEING CALLED "GRANDMA" BY STRANGERS AND RELATIVES (EXCEPT YOUR GRANDCHILDREN)?
The Liberated Grandmother Answers: "NO!"

The reason is simple.

When you lose your name, you lose your identity.

I want my identity.

Every successful grandmother *needs* her identity.

She has to be *herself.*

The grandmother myth turns you into a "typical grandmother." One typical grandmother is like another.

When a stranger or a distant relative calls you "Grandma," he's not seeing you as you. He's seeing a "typical grandmother."

Let your grandchildren call you "grandma." You *are their* grandma. But you're nobody else's.

And don't you forget it.

And when you're *yourself,* you can be the most wonderful person in the world.

§   §

An illustration. Let's suppose you're in the midst of an important business or community meeting. You're trying to persuade some darn difficult hard-nosed men and women that your way of doing things is right. If they respect you, you'll get your point across. If they don't, you're a loser. And just as you think you've got them in the palm of your hands, the door is flung open and some stranger snaps at you, "Hey, Grandma, you're double-parked."

Part III

TEN EASY STEPS TOWARD BECOMING A SUCCESSFUL LIBERATED GRANDMOTHER

TEN EASY STEPS TOWARD BECOMING A SUCCESSFUL LIBERATED GRANDMOTHER

Even now that you know how the grandmother myth is booby-trapping your life, you may be hesitant about exchanging the "typical grandmother role" for a *strange* new life *on your own*.

After all, when you accept being a typical grandmother—when you follow every dictate of the grandmother myth—almost all the actions and attitudes of your later years are determined for you; you seldom have to think for yourself at all.

If you choose to be a liberated grandmother, you'll find no rules to guide your relationships with your children and your grandchildren. You'll suddenly face the need to make decisions *for yourself* without any help from anybody. The liberated grandmother understands that there are only two things in life about which we have no choice: we are born and we die. Almost everything else we do between these two extremes requires a decision. Can *you* make the decisions? Take this one-minute test and find out. Your decision-making ability will determine your chances of becoming a successful liberated grandmother.

A one-minute test:
WHAT ARE YOUR CHANCES OF BECOMING A SUCCESSFUL LIBERATED GRANDMOTHER?
Check off the NO or YES answer lines to the following questions.

You'll find out what your answers mean in the paragraphs following these questions.

	YES	NO
1. Do you keep a clear head even when a variety of confusing choices are open to you?	——	——
2. Do you gather all the facts before you make a decision?	——	——
3. When you gather facts, do you make sure you're not looking only for facts that will slant the decision in favor of the choice you prefer?	——	——
4. When you've gathered all the facts and weighed them, do you always come to a decision (rather than say, "I just can't make up my mind")?	——	——
5. Are you ready to accept the hard fact that making a decision often involves compromises or sacrifices?	——	——
6. Do you accept those compromises and sacrifices without resentment?	——	——
7. Once you've come to a decision, do you feel satisfied or are you still disturbed because you're not sure whether you've done the right thing?	——	——
8. Do you put your decision into action immediately—with vigor and enthusiasm?	——	——
9. If your decision proves to be wrong, do you take it calmly and try to determine what went wrong (so you won't make the same mistake again)?	——	——
10. When you've made a wrong decision, have you the gumption to start all over and get to the right decision?	——	——

Here's what your answers mean:

If you answered all the questions YES, you're an excellent decision-maker; you'll be able to get along very well on your own as a liberated grandmother.

If you answered any questions NO, you have a weakness as a decision-maker. The greater the number of NO's you checked off, the greater the number of weaknesses. The weaker your decision-making ability, the poorer your chances of becoming a liberated grandmother. *But you can correct your weaknesses.* Here's how:

The next time you must make a decision, use this same test as a checklist. The questions from 1 through 10, checked off YES, are actually *ten steps for making a successful decision*

When you've learned how to master those ten small steps toward making a decision, you've taken your first giant step toward becoming a successful liberated grandmother.

Part IV

HOW TO TURN YOUR SELF-DOUBTS ABOUT BEING A LIBERATED GRANDMOTHER INTO FEELINGS OF SELF-WORTH

HOW TO TURN YOUR SELF-DOUBTS ABOUT BEING A LIBERATED GRANDMOTHER INTO FEELINGS OF SELF-WORTH

What do you want to be—a *typical* grandmother, a puppet, or a liberated grandmother, your own true self?

I know that you may still have self-doubts. And I know why.

In a world in which much of our prestige and dignity comes from a role in life which society accepts, the loss of such a role can be a blow to your feelings of self-worth. When you give up your role as a "typical grandmother," self-doubts are certain to crowd your mind. Become a successful liberated grandmother and turn self-doubts into self-worth by following this advice.

HOW TO TURN YOUR

SELF-DOUBTS	INTO	SELF-WORTH

1. *If I'm not considered a typical grandmother, how can I enjoy prestige without that role?*

Easy. For a while enjoy your new-found freedom doing what you please. Then: Use your freedom in different kinds of service for others: teaching? nursing? counseling? welcoming neighbors? visiting shut-ins? volunteering in a hospital? Or in service for yourself: cooking? gardening? taking classes? traveling? money-making? earning a college degree? Pick the one that makes you feel best. You'll recover self-esteem when people say, "What a wonderful role in life you have!"—and you know it's true.

2. *I'm afraid—won't I lose my drive and zest once I don't have to do all the chores of a typical grandmother?*

Yes, if you let yourself be "put out to pasture," and mope around doing nothing except watching TV and feeling sorry for yourself. Meaningful things to do are all around you. Get involved in work, hobbies, clubs, civic and political life, volunteerism. Join the senior power movement. Or enjoy your leisure in any way you like. Stay active physically and mentally —be useful to yourself and to others—and you'll never lose your zest and drive.

3. *Suppose I want part-time work—will my abilities be as good as before?*

Scientific studies show that grandmothers who go back to work often out-perform younger folks at the same tasks. You never lose your skills. A little practice, and you can start getting pats on the back again.

4. *What if I can't work up the emotional energy to adjust to a new way of life?*

You easily work up the energy if you decide what things make you happy—then make it your business to get them. There's nothing like setting goals to arouse your enthusiasm. And enthusiasm is magical in tapping stores of emotional energy you never thought you had.

5. *What will happen to my pride when people know I'm not a typical grandmother?*	If you adjust to your new freedom happily, people will envy you. That should make you proud to be you. If you're financially secure, loved and fill your time with interesting and useful things to do, you have plenty to be proud of.
6. *Won't people look down on me if I spend a lot of time on my hobbies instead of on my grandchildren?*	Hobbies will get you in touch with other hobbyists of all ages, broaden your interests, and make you a more knowledgeable, entertaining, helpful and happier grandmother. People and your grandchildren will respect your new expertise and admire you for your many new friendships.
7. *All these new problems at my age—isn't it a big worry?*	Yes, if you simply fuss and fret. But if you think your problems through, and see what can be done about them, and do it, you'll have nothing to worry about. Be a person who can think through a problem rather than worry about it.
8. *What if I fail at doing things right as a liberated grandmother?*	You could. But failure is bad only if you learn nothing from it. Apply what you learned to build a success the next time you try.

9. *Will my mental powers be strong enough to make the right decisions as a liberated grandmother?*

The mind doesn't wear out—it rusts out from lack of use. Your mental powers can stay as strong as ever—as long as you continue to use them.

10. *Being a typical grandmother is a kind of routine. Won't I feel like a fish out of water without a routine?*

Not if you schedule your day—*your* way. Try to include some useful work—voluntary or for pay. It's doing things, working at things, that make most men and women interesting—keeps them involved, curious, receptive. Instead of feeling like a fish out of water, you'll feel like a fish that escaped from a small pond into an exciting new ocean of life.

Part V

THE LIBERATED GRANDMOTHER'S BILL OF RIGHTS

1

YOU HAVE THE RIGHT—*to turn your grandmaternal routine into a "free-lance" activity*

Do "work at" being a grandmother your own way; in this activity you're your own boss. "Think out" and "feel out" problems—making your brain and your emotions work for you to come up with the happiest solutions. Start your "free-lance" activity as a grandmother today.

2

YOU HAVE THE RIGHT—*to help your grandchildren within the limits of your physical, emotional and financial strengths*

Do know your physical limitations in relation to your grandchildren, and never exceed those limitations.

Do know just how much childhood imagination and activity you can take; and when you've had enough, call it quits. Never overtax your emotions.

Do be realistic about giving money to your grandchildren. Your big income years are in the past. You're going to need the cash more than the children. But don't be a skinflint, either. Give when you can, what you can, for something your grandchildren need but may not be able to get otherwise. Or give just for the good old-fashioned joy of giving.

3

YOU HAVE THE RIGHT—*to teach your grandchildren, but only when they're ready to listen and their parents are willing*

Do wait until your grandchild is ready to listen to you before you begin to teach—those things that only you can teach. Readiness to learn is more important than a good teacher; anybody can teach once a child is ready. Be patient and understanding, and you'll know when the right time has arrived.

Do tell stories emphasizing what is beautiful in life. Give your grandchildren a dream world that is within the grasp of their experience, so they can be stimulated to make a real world of beauty for themselves as they grow older.

Do read aloud. Your grandchildren will learn about the pleasures of reading cuddled warmly in your arms. You'll open their minds to the whole great world of books.

Do communicate with your grandchildren in emotional language— words and gestures. It's your right to teach your grandchildren the many ways of expressing love.

Do be the family historian and archive keeper. Tell your grandchildren the story of the family's past, and bewitch them with mementos and photos from yesterday. Give them a sense of the family's continuity.

Do talk about the wonders of growing old in freedom. Without a personal acquaintance with graceful aging, growing old can be a struggle in a trackless land. Help prepare your grandchildren today for all of their tomorrows.

Do neglect the nitty-gritty of brushing teeth, shining shoes, and not coming home late for dinner. Those subjects are outside a grandmother's curriculum. Let the mother teach plodding, day-to-day affairs. *You* concentrate on teaching your grandchildren to reach for the stars.

4

YOU HAVE THE RIGHT—*to baby-sit or not to baby-sit, as you choose*

Do baby-sit only when you feel up to it, when you feel you'd like to, and when you're not overly inconvenienced by doing so.

Do baby-sit in *your* home preferably, not your children's. That's a matter of self-protection. In your children's home, your grandchild is likely to think, *"My* mother does it this way—so, grandma, don't you tell me to do it like *that,"* and the child will balk at your instructions. In your home, your grandchild knows *you're* the boss.

Do tell your children straight-out, "Please, don't take me for granted."

5

YOU HAVE THE RIGHT—*to go anywhere in the world you please when you please and stay as long as you like*

Do use your freedom from child-rearing to go anyplace, anytime, and live wherever you want to. Your time is today—make the most of it. And if making the most of it means traveling or relocating, don't hesitate. Your grandchildren are not anchors around your neck.

This is elementary, but typical grandmothers have a habit of forgetting it: Your children and grandchildren have long lifetimes ahead of them. *Your* years are limited. Make the best of them. You've *made* your sacrifices all your life. You have no emotional debts to pay. Let your only emotional output be a joyous self-fulfillment.

6

YOU HAVE THE RIGHT—*to love your grandchildren on your own terms*

Do get over the notion that you ought to love your grandchildren equally. It's impossible—and that's a fact of life.

Do give more of yourself to those grandchildren who need it most. And don't be afraid to hear one grandchild say, ''You do more for 'him' than you do for me.'' If the other child needs more, you *have* to do more for ''him.''

7

YOU HAVE THE RIGHT—*to be made happy by your grandchildren and their parents*

Do get used to the idea that love is a two-way street. In a healthy parent/grandchild/grandmother relationship, there are three important ways the children and grandchildren can express their love. These ways may not come naturally, so without any pussy-footing, come right out and say to your children, here are three things among many you can do to make me happy:

"*One. Telephone.* I love to hear about the grandchildren's lives." An occasional phone call is a joy, because it keeps you close without getting you involved in the nitty-gritty problems of daily living which you'd encounter if you shared living quarters. Grandmothers like to know about family plans, activities and accomplishments. But don't pry. Talk to your grandchildren's parents as if they were the dearest of friends. *Never* scold, complain, or get "touchy." Let your children come away from the call with a feeling of satisfaction because they brought you happiness. Have the grandchildren put their "two cents" in also. Some of the most exciting and imaginative conversations in my life have been held with young children on the phone.

Don't be caught in the 1-2-3 minute telephone trap. Reduced costs pay off for business calls, but for family calls, setting a short time-limit can be disastrous. When you make a call, *you* are in the mood to talk—and talk and talk. But is your child? your grandchild? They may not be. And if they're not, and you're watching the clock, by the time they've warmed up to a friendly chat, you're about to shut them up with a hasty good-bye. Result: Complaints like, "Why do you phone me if you don't want to talk?" Or, "You can always find time for (fill in any other member of the family), why not for me?" When you phone, don't cut it short. That could be a short-cut to misunderstandings.

"Two. *Be aware of my need for approval, and understand and appreciate my new activities.* Ask me about them. I'll be happy to tell you."

"Three. *I want letters from you and the children.*" Most grandmothers tell me that next to their own children and grandchildren, the most welcome sight at the door is the mailman. "The only disappointment greater than an empty mailbox in the morning," one grandmother confided, "is a mailbox crammed with junk mail. I want letters from my children and grandchildren. And I want them often." I don't know of any grandmother who doesn't feel the same way.

You can get all the mail you need from your children and grandchildren if you work at it. Start by writing letters to them. Make them chatty, newsy, warm and affectionate. Your children will certainly respond. And if your grandchildren don't know how—teach them. One of the richest gifts you can give them is the art of letter writing. Tell them that every time they write a letter to you—or to anybody they love—they give joy. And they'll receive joy from the letters that arrive in return. If you write the kind of letters I know are in your heart, your grandchildren will look forward to the mailman as eagerly as you do.

8

YOU HAVE THE RIGHT—*to be your own person, not just a Grandma*

Do realize you are a special kind of individual like no one else in the world. You've an "ego"—a particular "me"—which will not be silenced or denied. Typical grandmotherhood stifles that ego. It kills the "me" that sets you apart from all other people. When you free yourself from "typical grandmotherhood" you become a person. There's a great deal of difference between being treated by everybody like a grandmother or like a human being.

A grandmother has a better opportunity to be a liberated person than any other woman. A young unmarried woman building a career still bears inherent parental obligations. A wife and mother striving toward self-actualization still has natural responsibilities toward her growing family. But a grandmother is finally freed by nature. Her only ties arise from love. And her love is freely given.

If you've been playing the typical grandmother role, drop it. A whole new world of happy relationships will open to you as an individual. Most important, you'll get to like yourself *more*.

If you haven't played the typical grandmother role yet, *don't* start. The right to be your own person is sacred.

9

YOU HAVE THE RIGHT—*to self-esteem without being a typical grandmother*

Do face the hard fact that playing the "typical grandmother," with its heavy burden of responsibilities, is not only not easy, it's virtually impossible. (Yet, before you read this book, the chances are you took it for granted that typical grandmotherhood was something you could handle with no difficulty at all.) Most women fail at playing the typical grandmother. Since that's their only role in life—you can imagine what that failure does to their self-esteem.

Take just one example:

The grandmother myth requires the grandmother to do as much for her grandchildren as she was able to do for her children. She can *not* do it—as you know from reading these pages. What a blow to her self-esteem *that* is!

Do keep your self-esteem by *not* becoming the typical grand-mother—that eliminates the possibility of failure; *and* by *becom-* a liberated grandmother—that ensures your success as an individual.

§   §

Don't feel that a liberated grandmother washes her hands of all responsibilities to her family. She no more will do that than she will relinquish her give-and-take relationship with other human beings. The liberated grandmother knows that her wisdom and experience—and, yes, the special prestige that comes with being a liberated grandmother —can strongly influence the lives of every member of her family. As a peacemaker alone, she occupies a position that can be filled by no other member of the family. The liberated grandmother applies her new-found self to help solve her family's quarrels, difficulties, and problems. When she does that she earns the esteem of everyone—and of herself. Self-liberation is the key to self-esteem.

10

YOU HAVE THE RIGHT—*to build a new life for yourself without being judged by your children*

Do remember, you have the right to make of your life anything you want to make of it.

You *don't* become a different person the moment you become a grandmother. You *don't* become the "typical grandmother" of the grandmother myth—devoting the rest of your life to your grandchildren. You *don't* automatically turn into a self-sacrificing saint.

You remain *yourself*—With the same needs, prejudices, and feelings as before. If you want to *develop* your *self* along other lines than those laid down for the typical grandmother, there's no one in the world who has the right to judge you—least of all your children. It's *natural* for you to build a new life for yourself now that you're *free* from the responsibilities of child rearing.

How do you start building your new life?

Consider your life as a pie. When you're a baby, the whole pie belongs to you; you have no responsibilities to anybody. When you're four years old, you're sent to Sunday school; a slice of that pie goes for Sunday school, your new responsibility. Enter regular school, and another slice of the pie is taken from you. With each brother and sister born into the family, more and more slices of the pie disappear. Higher education gobbles up additional slices. Your marriage and your work-life scoop out almost all the remaining slices. Usually, becoming a grandmother wipes the pie-pan clean. You could be left with nothing of life's pie.

But now when you start your new liberated life, begin by being sure to keep a slice of life's pie *for yourself.*

Keep a part of yourself free from responsibilities. Keep a part of yourself *to* yourself. Keep something in your life important to you that has no connection with anybody else.

It's on this part of yourself—this vital part of yourself which isn't responsible to anybody or anything—that you can build your new life.

If you haven't consciously set that secret part of yourself aside, take a good hard look inside yourself. You'll find it there. Every woman has a dream of something she wants for herself and herself alone. *Now* is the time to transform that dream into reality. When you do, you'll find once again, the whole pie of life will be yours.

Act now! Your future is today!

Part VI

THE TEN COMMANDMENTS OF SUCCESSFUL LIBERATED GRANDMOTHERHOOD

THE TEN COMMANDMENTS FOR SUCCESSFUL LIBERATED GRANDMOTHERHOOD

You have the right to be a happy, fulfilled woman. You can become one by following these *Ten Commandments For Successful Liberated Grandmotherhood.*

1. *Do* take on tasks that you know are "do-able." (The tasks of a "typical grandmother" are *not.)*

2. *Do* valuable things with your time—and by that I mean things *valuable* to yourself. That means anything you enjoy doing and do well, not excluding making money.

3. *Do* start up a new happier relationship with your husband.

4. *Do* travel when the urge strikes you and stay as long as you like. And don't wait until it's too late.

5. *Do* relocate if it makes you feel better.

6. *Do* say "Yes" to requests by your children in the name of your grandchildren only when you're able, willing, and can afford it.

7. *Do* live as vigorous a sex life as you like.

8. *Do* make "grandmothering" a part of your life, but not all of it—and not the most important part of it.

9. *Do* teach your grandchildren (when they're ready to learn) about the heritage of your youth and the glories of your mature years.

10. *Do* develop yourself as an individual and become the woman you always wanted to be.

§   §

Becoming a happy fulfilled woman is the only way of becoming a successful grandmother. To demonstrate to your grandchildren the richness of life possible in one's golden years, you must live your own life. The glow of your happiness, the content of your self-fulfillment will be remembered by your grandchildren forever. You will always be to them a living proof of how wonderful life can be. They will want to make their lives just as wonderful. You can leave no greater legacy.